Dancing Around the World

Julie Nickerson

AF585049

Dancing Around the World

Text: Julie Nickerson
Publishers: Tania Mazzeo and Eliza Webb
Series consultant: Amanda Sutera
Hands on Heads Consulting
Editors: Jarrah Moore and Sarah Layton
Project editor: Annabel Smith
Designer: Leigh Ashforth
Project designer: Danielle Maccarone
Maps: Chellie Carroll
Permissions researcher: Lumina Datamatics
Production controller: Renee Tome

Acknowledgements
We would like to thank the following for permission to reproduce copyright material:

Front cover: iStock.com/Nikada; p. 4: IndiaPix/IndiaPicture/Getty Images; p. 5 (top): Michael Williams/Alamy Stock Photo, (bottom and p. 32): V&P Photo Studio/Adobe Stock Photos; p. 6: Horizon International Images/Alamy Stock Photo; p. 7 (top): Studio Romantic/Shutterstock.com, (bottom): iStock.com/diignat; p. 8: Jon Anders Wiken/Dreamstime.com; p. 9 (top): Vadim Petrakov/Shutterstock.com; (bottom): Andy Soloman/Shutterstock.com; p. 10 (top): AfriPics.com/Alamy Stock Photo, (bottom): Hugh Sitton/Stone/Getty Images; p. 11: Jiti Chadha/Alamy Stock Photo; p. 12: NARINDER NANU/AFP/Getty Images; p. 13: NurPhoto/NurPhoto/Getty Images; p. 14: Kobby Dagan/Shutterstock.com; p. 15 (top): Carl Court/Getty Images Entertainment/Getty Images, (bottom): Bruno Vincent/Getty Images News/Getty Images; p. 16: Lynnette Peizer/Alamy Stock Photo; p. 17: Buda Mendes/Getty Images News/Getty Images; p. 18: CARL DE SOUZA/AFP/Getty Images; p. 19: AFP/Getty Images; p. 20: Mondadori Portfolio/Getty Images; p. 21: (top): iStock.com/iStock Signature, (bottom): skynesher/E+/Getty Images; p. 22 (top): tarczas/Alamy Stock Photo, (bottom): Hans Neleman/Stone/Getty Images; p. 23: tarczas/Alamy Stock Photo; p. 24: Album/Alamy Stock Photo; p. 25 (top): Eddie Gerald/Alamy Stock Photo, (bottom): Dinodia Photos/Alamy Stock Photo; p. 26 (top): Volodymyr Melnyk/Alamy Stock Photo, (bottom): oneinchpunch/Shutterstock.com; p. 27: oneinchpunch/Shutterstock.com; p. 28: Igor Bulgarin/Shutterstock.com; p. 29: (top, bottom): Golden Pixels LLC/Alamy Stock Photo; p. 30: (top): Jack Vartoogian/Getty Images/Archive Photos/Getty Images, (bottom): Paul Cunningham - Corbis/Corbis Entertainment/Getty Images.

Every effort has been made to trace and acknowledge copyright. However, if any infringement has occurred, the publishers tender their apologies and invite the copyright holders to contact them.

NovaStar

Text © 2025 Cengage Learning Australia Pty Limited
Illustrations © 2025 Cengage Learning Australia Pty Limited

Copyright Notice
This Work is copyright. No part of this Work may be reproduced, stored in a retrieval system, or transmitted in any form or by any means without prior written permission of the Publisher. Except as permitted under the *Copyright Act 1968*, for example any fair dealing for the purposes of private study, research, criticism or review, subject to certain limitations. These limitations include: Restricting the copying to a maximum of one chapter or 10% of this book, whichever is greater; Providing an appropriate notice and warning with the copies of the Work disseminated; Taking all reasonable steps to limit access to these copies to people authorised to receive these copies; Ensuring you hold the appropriate Licences issued by the Copyright Agency Limited ("CAL"), supply a remuneration notice to CAL and pay any required fees.

ISBN 978 0 17 033495 2

Cengage Learning Australia
Level 5, 80 Dorcas Street
Southbank VIC 3006 Australia
Phone: 1300 790 853
Email: aust.nelsonprimary@cengage.com

For learning solutions, visit **cengage.com.au**

Printed in Malaysia by Papercraft
1 2 3 4 5 6 7 29 28 27 26 25

Nelson acknowledges the Traditional Owners and Custodians of the lands of all First Nations Peoples. We pay respect to Elders past and present, and extend that respect to all First Nations Peoples today.

Contents

Moving to the Music

People of all ages, all over the world, love to dance. Dancing is the movement of the body, usually while listening to music or a song.

Many dancers use movement to show emotions and tell stories. Fast movements can show excitement and slow movements can show sadness or fear. Dancers also communicate using facial expressions and hand **gestures**.

Some dance styles require special skills and movements. Others allow dancers to **improvise** and make up their own steps and performances. Dancers can dance solo (that is, on their own), in a duo (meaning with a partner), or in a group.

An Indian bhangra dancer performs a dance step with a *daang* stick.

Dancers often wear special clothing and shoes when they are dancing. These clothes are usually comfortable and easy to move in. For performances, sometimes dancers wear special costumes. They may also use props such as umbrellas, scarves or swords to help them tell their story through dance.

Most indoor dance spaces are large and have a hard floor. Music or songs usually **accompany** a dance, and sometimes the musicians and singers are part of the performance.

Chinese dancers perform with paper umbrellas during Moon Festival celebrations.

Hold That Pose!

Dancers sometimes communicate by not moving at all! Becoming still during a dance can create a feeling of suspense or excitement.

Why People Dance

People dance for many reasons. Personal reasons could be to have fun, to exercise and to be creative. Dance allows people to share and experience emotions and ideas. Dancing can help build self-confidence, and it can be used to share joy.

Dances can also be performed for cultural reasons. The dances may be traditions or part of celebrations. Some traditional dances tell stories of the past and some celebrate hard work or special times of the year. These dances are sometimes performed in front of an audience, or may only be shared with family and community members.

Lardil men dance at a corroboree (a ceremonial meeting) on Mornington Island, Queensland, in Australia.

For some people, dancing is a job. Professional dancers perform for audiences and sometimes travel to other cities or countries to share their performance. Some dancers work as dance teachers or choreographers.

You can go to dance classes run by a professional dance teacher.

Choreographers

Choreographers are people who create dances set to specific songs or pieces of music. They choose the movements and positions for each dancer. They can change the speed of the dance or how large the dancers' movements will be to communicate different emotions.

Traditional Dances

A traditional dance is a dance style performed by people from a particular culture. Some of these dances have been around for hundreds of years!

Adumu – Kenya and Tanzania

The adumu dance is performed by the Maasai people of Kenya and Tanzania in East Africa. Dancing has always been an important part of Maasai culture and is used in many events to celebrate different stages of life.

One of the occasions where adumu is performed is the Eunoto ceremony. This is a **rite of passage** that marks when young men become adult Maasai warriors by showing their power and strength to their community.

Young Maasai men perform an adumu dance.

The dance involves Maasai men coming together in a circle. They take turns to step forward and jump high into the air, giving the dance its commonly used name of the "Jumping Dance". It is a competitive dance – the higher the jump, the stronger and braver the warrior is. This sounds like a simple dance, but it is not!

A Maasai warrior jumps high up into the air.

To jump high, the dancers need strong leg muscles and good balance. Keeping their arms at their sides, they bounce slightly and then jump straight upwards. They repeat the jump as many times as they can, with their heels staying off the ground between jumps. Maasai boys train for this very **strenuous** dance from a young age.

As the dancers take turns to jump, the other men, as well as other community members, sing and chant in the background. They sing loudly to encourage each dancer to jump as high as they can. This singing and dancing can last for hours.

The whole Maasai community is involved in the adumu dance.

The Maasai men wear a traditional cloth called a *shuka* for the ceremony. It is usually a red fabric which is wrapped around the dancer's body and tied into a knot. They often wear colourful necklaces made of beads or shells. Some dancers carry wooden sticks or spears during the dance as a symbol of their bravery.

The adumu dance is also performed at weddings and other events. It is popular with tourists from other countries, who enjoy watching this show of energy and power.

A Maasai *moran* (warrior) in traditional dress holds a spear.

The adumu dance remains an important part of Maasai culture that is passed down to younger generations.

How High?

Some Maasai men can jump about 50 centimetres into the air! This is much higher than the average adult can jump.

Bhangra – India and Pakistan

Bhangra is a dance that comes from the Punjab **region** of India and Pakistan. It was first performed by **Punjabi** farmers as a celebration of hard work and a successful **harvest**. Originally, the dance was only performed by men.

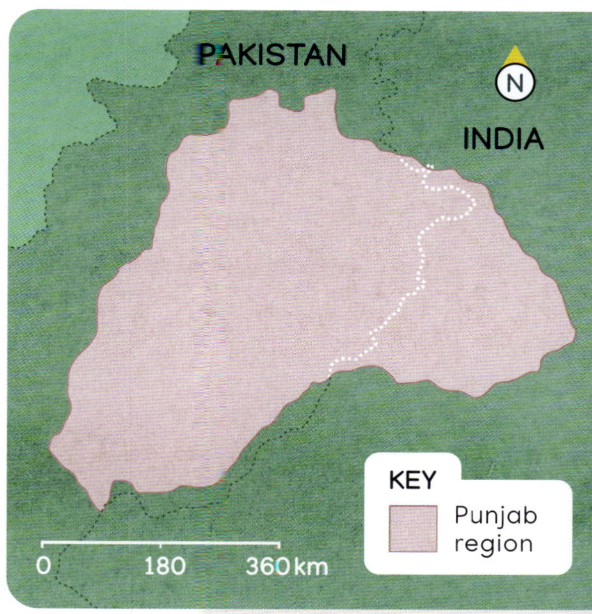

During the 1940s, bhangra dancing started to spread into other regions. It was first performed on a stage in front of an audience in the 1950s. Bhangra is now performed by both men and women, often in large groups.

A bhangra dance group performs in the town of Kila Raipur in Punjab, India.

Music and song accompany bhangra dancing. Traditionally, a special drum called a *dhol* provides the beat.

Bhangra dancing is very energetic. Dancers often dance in **unison** and move together around the dance space. They use big arm and shoulder movements and fast **footwork**. Dancers must be very fit, with movements including bending, jumping and kicking. Bhangra is a dance of celebration, and dancers show this with happy facial expressions. They sometimes use props such as poles and instruments when they are dancing.

Young men and women perform a bhangra dance with a dhol drum in Amritsar, India.

Bhangra dancers wear bright, colourful clothes. They wear a long, loose cloth around their waist and a long shirt that sometimes has a waistcoat over the top. Male dancers wear a **turban** and female dancers wear a long scarf called a *dupatta*, which wraps around their neck or shoulders and over the top of their head. Necklaces and earrings are worn to bring attention to the dancer's facial expressions. Bhangra dancers usually dance barefoot.

Bhangra is now a popular dance in many countries. It is seen in competitions, **Bollywood movies** and at family celebrations such as birthdays and weddings. It is also now a popular way to exercise all over the world.

Two women perform a bhangra dance to help showcase Punjabi culture in Edmonton, Canada.

Folk Dancing

Bhangra is a type of folk dance. These are dances that represent a part of the daily life of people from a certain area. Folk dances are passed down from one generation to the next and are often used in celebrations.

Kabuki – Japan

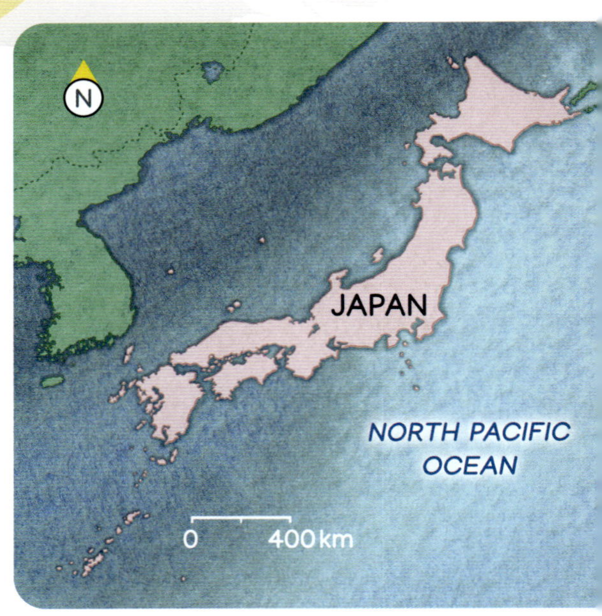

Kabuki is a kind of **theatrical** performance that was created in Japan in the 1600s. Earlier types of Japanese theatre were performed in front of royalty, but kabuki was intended to provide entertainment for people from all parts of society.

Kabuki tells stories through dance, music, acting and song. The stories can be about love, conflict or events in history. Sometimes they are comical.

Kabuki dancers are known for their costumes and very expressive faces.

Kabuki performances can be very exciting. Some performances include dramatic fight scenes performed by the dancers. Kabuki stages often have a long walkway that extends into the theatre, giving the audience a thrilling close-up view of the drama. Entering and exiting the stage can be an important part of the kabuki performance, with performers sometimes appearing or disappearing through trapdoors in the floor! In particular parts of the performance, the audience is invited to participate by calling out to encourage the performers.

A kabuki dancer performs in a show in Tokyo.

Kabuki dancers often wear traditional **kimono** and large wigs. The heavy kimono can limit their ability to make large movements or take big steps. Holding props such as fans, umbrellas, flowers and swords allows the dancers to create larger movements and patterns in the air. Many kabuki dancers wear white make-up on their faces and necks to highlight their facial expressions.

A kabuki dancer wears a traditional kimono and wig.

Kabuki dancers are also able to communicate with small movements, such as making shuffling movements with their feet or tilting their heads. An important part of the kabuki performance is when a dancer stops moving and stares at the audience. This draws the audience's attention to their character.

Kabuki musicians play the *shamisen* during a performance.

Kabuki musicians and singers sit on the stage during the dance performance. They play instruments such as the Japanese flute, drums and a stringed instrument called a *shamisen*.

Men Only

Kabuki was originally performed by women. However, in 1629, the Japanese government banned women from performing. Since then, traditional kabuki dancing is only performed by men, who play both male and female characters.

Samba – Brazil

The samba is the most popular dance in Brazil. It is a traditional dance that has been around since the late 1800s. There are several versions of the dance.

The most famous version of the samba is called "samba no pé". It is performed in street parades during the annual Brazilian Carnival, which is held before the start of **Lent**. The biggest Carnival parade is in the city of Rio de Janeiro. It attracts millions of visitors every year!

Samba no Pé

"Pé" (pronounced *peh*) means "foot" in Portuguese, which is the main language of Brazil. "Samba no pé" means "samba on the feet".

A samba dancer performs during Rio de Janeiro's 2024 Carnival in Brazil.

The Carnival parades include dancers from samba schools across the country. They spend many months rehearsing and preparing their costumes.

Samba dancers wear brightly decorated costumes, including large headdresses made with long feathers and colourful beads. Dancers wear bright, glittery make-up, and it can take several hours for them to get ready. Samba no pé is a solo dance, but many dancers get together to do it at the same time at Carnival.

Members of a samba school perform on the first night of Rio de Janeiro's Carnival parade in Brazil, 2022.

Dancers hold their bodies straight for the samba, and move their feet in fast, small steps. They use large arm movements and strong facial expressions. During Carnival parades, they may dance for several hours, so dancers need to be very fit.

Samba music is very lively. Drummers and other musicians follow the dancers down the street during Carnival.

Samba on the Move

During Carnival parades, some dancers perform on floats. These are spectacular stages which can be driven slowly down the street. They are decorated to reflect the theme of the Carnival.

Enormous crowds line the edges of the road in Rio de Janeiro's special parade area to watch the Carnival floats.

Popular Dance Styles

Today, there are many popular dance styles that are taught in classes all over the world.

Ballet

Ballet was created in Italy in the 1400s. It is now performed and enjoyed by people worldwide.

Ballet dancing requires precise movements, positions and skills. Dancers need to be flexible, fit and have good balance. Male ballet dancers may have to lift or catch female dancers, so they need to be very strong.

During classes, ballet dancers wear tight-fitting clothes such as leotards and tights. These are easy to move in and allow the teacher to check for correct body positions. For performances, dancers wear a variety of costumes. The most well-known costume for female ballet dancers is called a "tutu".

A male ballet dancer lifts another dancer into the air.

Ballet classes usually take place in large rooms called studios. These studios have floor-to-ceiling mirrors, making it easy for dancers to check their positions. The dancers can hold a wooden rail called a "barre" (pronounced *bar*) to help them balance while practising.

Young dancers practise their positions in a ballet studio with help from a teacher.

Tip of the Toe

Female ballet dancers often wear footwear called "pointe shoes". These give the dancer support while allowing her to dance and spin on the tips of her toes.

Ballroom

Ballroom dancing is performed by a pair, or duo. Ballroom dancing began in Europe in the 1500s. Today, there are ballroom dancing classes, events and competitions held worldwide.

There are many types of ballroom dances, including the tango, cha-cha and foxtrot. One of the most well-known ballroom dances is the waltz.

Ballroom dances follow a set **sequence** of steps, with partners spinning, turning and stepping together. Ballroom dances may be performed at weddings, formal events and other social occasions. Music for the dance is provided by a live band at some events. The music can be fast or slow, depending on the dance.

A dance duo perform a slow waltz in a competition.

A ballroom dancing duo dances the tango.

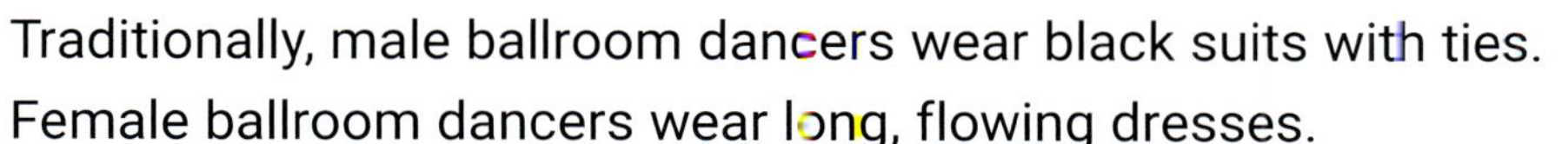

Traditionally, male ballroom dancers wear black suits with ties. Female ballroom dancers wear long, flowing dresses.

Round They Go

When there are many pairs dancing quickly around the dance floor, they all move in an anti-clockwise direction so they do not crash into each other!

Ballroom dancers move in an anti-clockwise direction around a competition dance floor.

Bollywood

Bollywood dancing is used in many Bollywood movies from India to tell part of the movie's story. By the 1950s, dancing had become a spectacular feature of Bollywood movies, and Bollywood dancing is still very popular today. Modern Bollywood dancing has been influenced by many dance styles, including bhangra, disco, jazz and hip-hop.

Bollywood dances are energetic and usually involve many dancers. Dancers often use large body movements and strong facial expressions to tell a story. They sing and dance to background music. These dances are very dramatic with lots of twirling, spinning movements that make their colourful clothing and jewellery swirl through the air.

Bollywood dancers perform in the 2012 film *Agneepath.*

Teams of people work together to produce Bollywood dance scenes. The teams have to consider aspects of the performance such as the dance space, camera angles, lighting, props, music and costumes. Bollywood choreographers work with the dancers throughout rehearsals and filming.

The crew gets ready to film a dance sequence in a studio in Mumbai, India.

Mudra

Bollywood dancers use many hand gestures when they dance. Traditional hand gestures from Indian classical dances are called *mudra*, and each has a special meaning.

Hip-Hop

Hip-hop is a type of street dance that was created in New York, the USA, in the 1970s and became popular through the 1980s and 1990s.

Hip-hop dancers often wear loose, baggy pants and large shirts so that they can move easily. They wear sneakers that keep their feet from slipping on the floor during fast movements.

Popping is done by tensing the muscles and then quickly releasing them, causing a small movement.

This dance style requires good balance, strength and fitness. There are many large, powerful movements that involve both the upper and lower body. Two of the most common hip-hop moves are "popping" and "locking". Hip-hop dancing also allows dancers to improvise and express themselves through the dance.

A group of hip-hop dancers is usually called a "crew".

Hip-hop dancing is performed to hip-hop and rap music. It can be performed solo or in groups. There are many hip-hop dance competitions held internationally every year.

Lock It In

The hip-hop move called "locking" was invented by accident in the 1960s, when dancer Don Campbell from the USA forgot his dance steps and stopped suddenly, "locking" himself into a still position. Today, hip-hop dancers use locking often, suddenly "freezing" in a particular pose between fast movements.

The Joy of Dancing

People dance for many reasons and in many different ways. Dancers may wear comfortable clothing or they may dress in special costumes. Some dancers train for years to learn a certain dance, and others improvise and create their own dances. To perform longer or difficult dances, dancers need to be fit, strong and flexible. Whether it's in class, on a stage, at a festival or celebration or at home with friends and family, people around the world use dancing to tell a story, show their emotions or simply share joy.

We can all tell stories through dance, by ourselves or with friends.

A BACKSTAGE PASS TO THE BALLET

by Zana

My class went on a special excursion to watch the ballet today. We also went backstage to learn about professional ballet performances.

First, we met the choreographer out on the stage. She told us about the work that happens long before the performance, such as **auditions** and rehearsals. She also talked about the importance of costumes and stage lighting to help bring the ballet's story to life.

We went backstage next and saw the dressing rooms where the dancers get their hair and make-up done. We watched some of the dancers warming up before the performance. Many were stretching and practising positions on the barre.

Then we took our seats with the rest of the audience. The theatre was huge, and we had great seats close to the stage. Large curtains hid the stage from view.

Finally, the music started and the curtains opened. The dancers burst onto the stage from both sides. I was surprised that there were so many of them on the stage at once! They danced together in perfect time to the music.

Some of the dancers' movements were slow and graceful, and these made me feel a bit sad. Others were energetic and playful, with dancers jumping high into the air. The ballet was made up of several dances and each had different costumes and lighting. Together, the dances and music told a story about a girl who was under a magic spell, and how she became free.

In the final dance, the music became louder and faster, the lighting became brighter and the dancing became more powerful. I could tell from the dancers' faces and movements that it was a dance of joy. I clapped very loudly when it was over!

My favourite part was when one of the male dancers lifted a female dancer high into the air and carried her across the stage. It looked like she was flying.

I can't wait to see another ballet performance. Maybe I'll go with my family next time!

Glossary

accompany (*verb*)	to occur with something else
auditions (*noun*)	short performances dancers must do to apply for a role in a performance or a dance group
Bollywood movies (*noun*)	movies made in India that often have parts where the characters sing and dance together
footwork (*noun*)	the way a dancer moves their feet in a dance
gestures (*noun*)	movements made with the body to convey a particular meaning
harvest (*noun*)	crops that have been cut and gathered on a farm when they are ready to eat and sell
improvise (*verb*)	to decide what dance movements to make on the spot instead of planning them
unison (*noun*)	all together at the same time
kimono (*noun*)	a traditional piece of Japanese clothing that is like a long dress with wide sleeves
Lent (*noun*)	a period each year when some Christian people give up something of value to them
Punjabi (*adjective*)	from the Punjab region, or area, of India and Pakistan
region (*noun*)	a large area of land that usually doesn't have exact borders
rite of passage (*noun*)	a special ceremony or event when a person reaches an important stage of life, such as becoming an adult
sequence (*noun*)	a series of events, such as dance steps, with a particular order
strenuous (*adjective*)	needing a lot of effort
theatrical (*adjective*)	to do with acting on stage
turban (*noun*)	a long piece of cloth wrapped around the head

Index